Jam Session

Kevin Garnett

Terri Dougherty
ABDO Publishing Company

visit us at
www.abdopub.com

Published by ABDO Publishing Company, 4940 Viking Drive, Suite 622, Edina, Minnesota 55435.
Copyright © 1999 by Abdo Consulting Group, Inc. International copyrights reserved in all countries.
No part of this book may be reproduced in any form without written permission from the publisher.

Printed in the United States.

Cover and Interior Photo credits: AP/Wide World Photos

Edited by Denis Dougherty

Sources: Minneapolis Star Tribune; NBA Inside Stuff; Sports Illustrated; Sports Illustrated For Kids;
The Sporting News; USA Today

Library of Congress Cataloging-in-Publication Data

Dougherty, Terri.
    Kevin Garnett / Terri Dougherty.
    p. cm. -- (Jam Session)
    Includes index.
    Summary: Examines the life and basketball career of the man who joined the Minnesota
Timberwolves in 1995, when he was only nineteen.
    ISBN 1-57765-039-5 (hardcover)
    ISBN 1-57765-341-6 (paperback)
    1. Garnett, Kevin, 1976- --Juvenile literature. 2. Basketball players--United States--
Biography--Juvenile literature. [1. Garnett, Kevin, 1976- . 2. Basketball players.
3. Afro-Americans--Biography.] I. Title. II. Series.
GV884.G37D68 1999
796.323'092--dc21
    [B]
                                                    98-7626
                                                       CIP
                                                            AC

Contents

Leader of the Wolves Pack

Kevin Garnett knew it was time for "The Kid" to be "The Man." The 21-year-old Minnesota Timberwolves all-star had just heard some bad news. The team's leading scorer, Tom Gugliotta, would probably miss the rest of the 1997-98 NBA season because of an ankle injury.

The Timberwolves had lost two games in a row and were facing the veteran Houston Rockets in an important late February game.

That night, before a screaming crowd at Minneapolis' Target Center, Kevin showed he was mature beyond his years. The 6-foot, 11-inch forward did nearly everything a basketball player could do in leading his team to a 100-95 overtime victory.

Wearing his baggy shorts and No. 21 jersey, he brought the ball up the court. He passed to teammates for open shots. He made jump shots over Charles Barkley. He outfought Hakeem Olajuwon and Barkley for rebounds. On defense, Kevin used his long arms to force Clyde Drexler into missing layups. He guarded centers, forwards, and guards.

Kevin finished with 25 points, a game-high 17 rebounds, 4 assists, and 2 blocked shots. More importantly, like all true superstars, he was at his best when it mattered most—in the fourth quarter and overtime. Barkley said after the game, "That kid is unbelievable!"

He brought the crowd to its feet when he rebounded missed shots with emphatic dunks. He saved a ball from going out of bounds and flipped it to a teammate for a basket.

More than anything, he just had fun. He pointed to teammates when they made a good play, got the crowd fired up, and played with enthusiasm. The fans, especially those in the "K.G.'s Krazies" section and all the kids wearing No. 21 jerseys, roared their approval. As he had been his entire life, he was at home on the basketball court.

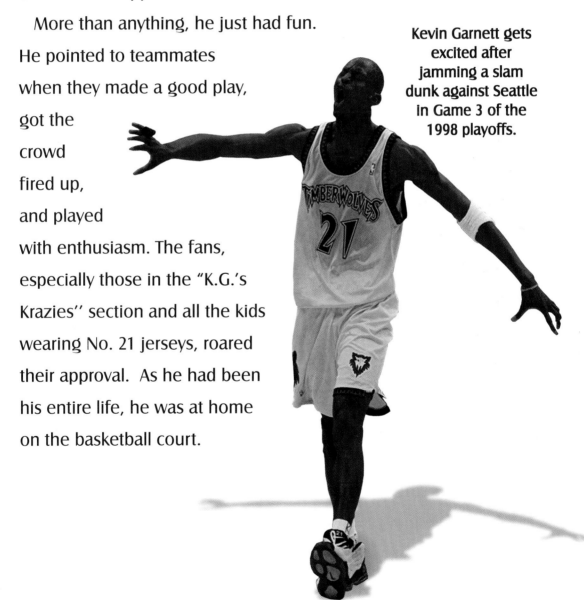

Kevin Garnett gets excited after jamming a slam dunk against Seattle in Game 3 of the 1998 playoffs.

Practice, Practice

Thirteen-year-old Kevin Garnett's eyes were glued to the TV. He was watching, and he was studying. He was watching Magic Johnson of the Los Angeles Lakers pass the ball with a perfect touch.

Then Kevin grabbed his basketball and called his best friend, Jamie "Bug" Peters. It was time to practice what he had seen.

Jamie lived across the street from Kevin in Mauldin, South Carolina, a city of hilly streets and magnolia trees. Kevin and his family had moved to Mauldin from nearby Greenville when he was 12. He and Jamie had quickly become good friends and spent many hours playing basketball at Springfield Park.

Garnett slaps away a shot by Cleveland Cavaliers guard Derek Anderson (23).

Kevin wanted to learn all he could about the game. Basketball was his life.

"All he did was talk about basketball," Baron Franks, who often played with Kevin, said. "Every time you saw him, he had a ball."

Kevin always thought about getting better. He talked about playing in college and hoped to become a professional basketball player. Little did he know his dream would come true sooner than he expected.

K.G. rocks the arena.

The Mauldin Marvel

*B*asketball was Kevin's game at Mauldin High School. He loved it, and it showed. When he was a freshman he was 6-foot-7 and already a good player. He averaged 12.5 points, 14 rebounds, and 7 blocks per game. But before his sophomore year, something changed that made him even better.

That summer at a basketball camp, he played harder. He had more confidence. He worked on settling down and concentrating. More importantly, he was directing other players on his team. He was becoming a leader. His presence could pull a team together.

While Kevin's height gave him an advantage over smaller players, it was also awkward for him sometimes. He had to learn how to maneuver his lanky body.

Kevin's friends at the park teased him that he was over 6 1/2 feet tall and couldn't dunk the ball! But he kept improving. Even in high school, Kevin had a feel for making the big play. He wasn't selfish. He loved to pass to his teammates.

"He didn't care who scored," James "Duke" Fisher, Mauldin High School's coach, said. "The only thing he hated was to lose."

Fisher taught Kevin a lot about dribbling, passing, and shooting. But practice is what made Kevin's skills get better. "He'd leave one practice and go practice again," Fisher said. "I never saw someone so obsessed."

After the high school season, Kevin would play for an Amateur Athletic Union team. He laughed and kidded around with his teammates. When he made a big play he would let out a yell because he was having such a good time. While he was having fun he was also winning. In 1994, his amateur team won the Kentucky Hoopfest tournament in Louisville.

During his junior year in high school Kevin began to attract attention from college coaches. He averaged 27 points, 17

K.G. would practice for hours every day after school.

rebounds, and 7 blocks per game. His team went 22-7 and the Mauldin Mavericks made it to the upper-state championship in March 1994.

When Kevin played, people noticed. The high school gym in Mauldin would be packed with spectators, and people would stand in the hall just to listen to the game. Kids would ask him for his autograph.

But all the attention made Kevin uncomfortable. Basketball put him in the spotlight.

Kevin Garnett goes for the big slam during a game with Farragut Academy.

A Move to Chicago

By September of Kevin's senior year in high school his family had moved to Chicago. He attended Farragut Academy on Chicago's west side.

Kevin had to make new friends at the school. But he knew the basketball coach, and quickly fit in with his new teammates. He became known as "Da Kid" in a city famous for rooting for "Da Bears" and "Da Bulls."

"The first time my group of guys met Kevin and played with him, it was like they'd been playing together for years," said William Nelson, Farragut's head coach. "Kevin was a born leader. Even though he is so good, his personality is to come in, be humble, and do whatever he has to do to fit in."

At Farragut, Kevin averaged 25.2 points, 17.9 rebounds, 6.7 assists, and 6.5 blocked shots per game. He helped Farragut win 28 of its first 29 games and reach the Final 8 of the Class AA state tournament at Champaign.

To get to state, Farragut had to win the tough Chicago Public League tournament. Kevin didn't seem to feel the pressure. He had 32 points and 13 rebounds in the championship game as Farragut defeated Chicago Carver 71-62.

'Da Kid' Shines

"**K**evin's ability, unselfishness, and work ethic set him apart from other talented players", said his coach, who has seen many great players in the Chicago area over the years. Nelson sometimes had to tell Kevin to shoot more, instead of passing so often.

"He was so unselfish, trying to get other players involved," Nelson recalled. "So many other superstar players are selfish."

Kevin knew what it took to win. He would sometimes start practice and make the players sweat through drills before the coach arrived!

"He was the hardest worker I've ever seen," Nelson said. "I never thought anyone could be that intense."

Word about Kevin and the Farragut team spread quickly. The Farragut games were crowded with spectators and reporters.

"It was a crazy year," Nelson said. "There were cameras everywhere. Newspapers covered us like we were the Bulls sometimes, and every TV channel you turned on had highlights of the Farragut game."

Despite the team's popularity, the season ended in disappointment. At the state tournament, top-ranked Farragut was upset 46-43 by Harvey Thornton in the quarterfinals. Kevin's three-point attempt bounced off the rim just before the buzzer. He had 17 points and 16 rebounds in the game.

Kevin was named to the all-tournament team and selected as Illinois' "Mr. Basketball." In the McDonald's High School All-American Game, he had 18 points and 11 rebounds and earned MVP honors.

Kevin Garnett playing for Farragut Academy in 1995.

"He's the most complete player I've ever seen at any level," Nelson said. "Even the old-timers around here say they've never seen anything like that."

The loss in the tournament wasn't the only disappointment Kevin had during his senior year. In order to play college basketball at the highest level, he had to do more than play basketball well. He also had to pass an important test.

Kevin studied hard for his college test and didn't miss classes. He stayed away from drugs and gangs and kept his focus on basketball. But reading was hard for him. He learned best by listening. The test involved a lot of reading and was standing between Kevin and college basketball. He tried hard, but he didn't pass.

"Man, I wanted to go to college," Kevin said. "I went to class. I wanted to have options."

In his mind, he had only one choice if he were to realize his dream of making basketball his career. He would take a chance at making it on a professional team.

He graduated from high school, and a few weeks later was in the 1995 NBA draft.

Rookie Kevin Garnett shows what he can do.

On the Way to the NBA

*I*n a college gym in Chicago, Kevin showed NBA scouts what he could do. It was three weeks before the draft. It was his chance to prove he was ready to be a professional, even though he was only 19 years old.

During the workouts, Kevin confidently showed off his special ability. One person who watched in awe of him was the Minnesota Timberwolves' vice president of basketball operations Kevin McHale.

McHale had a plan before he saw Kevin practice. McHale's plan was to spread the word that this kid was unbelievable and would be a star in the NBA. McHale was hoping that another team would pick him early and the Timberwolves could get a great player who had played college ball with their fifth pick.

After seeing Garnett practice McHale left the gym and never said a word. He hoped that Kevin would still be around when the Timberwolves' turn would come—he knew that Kevin had the tools to be a true superstar in the NBA.

His shooting, jumping, quickness, and ball handling amazed McHale. Kevin, however, didn't care which team he played for. He was grateful to have the chance to play in the NBA.

"Wherever I go it'll be an opportunity," Kevin said before the draft. "Millions of kids want to play pro basketball, and here I am getting the chance early. I learned one thing—never hate a positive option."

Draft day arrived and Kevin listened intently as teams made their selections. Joe Smith went to Golden State. Antonio McDyess went to the Los Angeles Clippers, who immediately traded him to Denver. Philadelphia took Jerry Stackhouse. And Rasheed Wallace was chosen by Washington.

Then it was time for the Minnesota Timberwolves to make their choice. He heard his name! Kevin smiled. He was headed for the NBA!

Kevin McHale, right, is excited about his new player Kevin Garnett.

"I was always on the outside looking in, wondering what it would be like," Kevin said. "Now I'm on the inside and I'm about to find out."

Beating the Odds

While he was honored to be playing in the NBA, Kevin knew it wouldn't be easy. The odds were against him.

The Timberwolves had raised some eyebrows by taking a young, unproven player with the fifth pick of the draft. Only one player had become a superstar in the pros without going to college. Moses Malone, one of the best rebounders ever, led the Philadelphia 76ers to the 1983 NBA title.

Although he was 19, Kevin's body still had some growing to do. He was almost seven feet tall, but very thin. He would be playing against men who were stronger and heavier.

And he would be growing up in the spotlight. He would have a lot of money—he signed a three-year contract worth more than $5 million—and the problems and responsibilities that come with it.

His first NBA coach was enthusiastic about Kevin's ability to learn to play in the pros.

"He's bright," coach Bill Blair said. "He picks things up as quickly as any rookie I've ever coached, and that includes Michael Jordan when I was with Chicago."

Kevin was optimistic. He didn't think going to the pros would be as hard as some thought. "It's basketball," he said. "I went with my heart. No regrets. No looking back."

Kevin found a big supporter in Kevin McHale. McHale played on three NBA championship teams. He appeared in seven all-star games in 13 seasons with the Boston Celtics. He knew Kevin had the potential to be a superstar.

"Sometimes you have to wait on greatness," McHale said. "He knows how to play."

The Wolves' Terry Porter, a veteran guard who had twice helped Portland to the NBA Finals, said, "I've always looked at college like it's the best four years of your life. But if he had gone to college, it would have been like a man against boys on the court."

K.G. heads toward the basket.

Introducing 'Da Kid'

*I*t was the 12th game of Kevin's rookie season and the Timberwolves seemed tired. The Wolves were playing the Vancouver Grizzlies at the Target Center.

The Wolves, 2-9 on the season, looked like they were playing the game in slow motion. Then Kevin caught a pass behind the three-point line. He tossed it toward the hoop. SWISH!

A smiling Kevin let out a howl that woke up the team and the crowd. The Timberwolves won 121-98, the team's biggest margin of victory in almost three years. He energized the team.

"His enthusiasm toward the game is something special," Sean Rooks, the Wolves' former backup center, said. "He gets pleasure out of playing."

Kevin was playing for a Timberwolves team that had been searching for a star. The team played its first game in 1989 and had never made the playoffs. The Timberwolves had a high draft choice every year, taking players such as Isaiah Rider, Christian Laettner, and Donyell Marshall, but none had been able to propel the team above mediocrity.

The Timberwolves won only 15 of their first 51 games during Kevin's first season. At the all-star break in February, he was averaging 21 minutes, 6.4 points, and 4.2 rebounds per game.

At times his ability shone. In a February game against defending NBA champion Houston, he scored nine straight points, grabbed two rebounds and blocked two shots during a two-minute stretch in the fourth quarter. He turned a tight game into a blowout that the Timberwolves won 120-101. He had 17 points, 12 rebounds, and 3 blocks in the game.

But he also made rookie mistakes. In the closing seconds of an overtime game against Golden State in January, Kevin was 11 feet (3.4 m) from the basket when he caught a pass from Tom Gugliotta. The Wolves were behind by a point. But instead of making a basket, he shot an airball. The Wolves lost 122-119.

"At the time it was disappointing," Kevin said. "But I had never been in that position before, on that level. I didn't really think I was going to get the ball. I wasn't ready. I can't worry about it."

Kevin worked hard at his new job. He was always the first at practice and got along well with his teammates. In his first year he broke the team record for blocked shots in a season, with 131.

In February he became a starter when Laettner was traded to Atlanta. Three weeks later he scored 33 points against the Celtics, a career high.

Kevin started the Wolves' final 42 games and averaged 14 points, 8.4 rebounds, and 2.26 blocks, shooting 53.3 percent from the field. He was named to the NBA's All-Rookie Second Team.

"He gets better every night," former NBA player and now basketball announcer Doc Rivers said. "But it's more than that. This kid has style."

Minnesota Timberwolves rookie Kevin Garnett takes it seriously when told to smile for official photos during media day.

A Little Help from His Friend

The summer before his senior year Kevin met another high school hoops star, point guard Stephon Marbury. They had developed a special friendship over the phone. They talked so often that half the money Kevin earned at a fast-food restaurant went toward his phone bills!

After three years of phone calls, they finally had a chance to play together in a summer All-Star Game. In a gym on Chicago's west side, Marbury lobbed a pass toward the basket. Kevin grabbed the ball over the rim. SLAM-DUNK! A perfect play!

The two dreamed of one day playing together in the NBA. That dream came true in Kevin's second year with the Timberwolves.

Kevin's buddy, Stephon Marbury, joined the Timberwolves in 1996.

The Timberwolves traded with the Milwaukee Bucks on draft day to get Marbury, who had starred at Georgia Tech for a year.

With Garnett and Marbury leading the way, the Timberwolves were getting better. They finished the season with a 40-42 record. They made the playoffs for the first time ever!

Kevin had a great year. He was getting more comfortable in the NBA. He was earning respect because of the way he played and conducted himself.

"He can be as good as he wants to be," Barkley said.

Kevin appeared in the NBA All-Star Game for the first time, and started 77 games. He missed five games in December with a sprained left foot. He was still able to break his own team single-season record for blocked shots with 163.

In his first playoff game, Kevin had 21 points and 9 rebounds against Houston. The veteran Rockets, however, swept the three-game series. Kevin averaged 17.3 points, 9.3 rebounds, and 3.7 assists in his first-ever playoff series.

The Timberwolves saw Kevin as their hope for the future. They confirmed their faith in him with a six-year contract extension for $125 million!

Coach Flip Saunders called Kevin, "Our team leader, our spiritual leader."

Up, Up and Away

Kevin continued his climb up the NBA ladder during the 1997-98 season. His talent and popularity with the fans was evident when he was voted a starter in the NBA All-Star Game.

At the All-Star Game in New York's historic Madison Square Garden, Kevin showed his all-around ability and unselfishness. Kevin was sharing the court with superstars Michael Jordan and Karl Malone. But if he was nervous, he didn't show it. He was having fun.

He scored 12 points, making 6 of 11 field-goal attempts, in 21 minutes. He had one of the most spectacular plays of the game, a one-handed windmill dunk in the third quarter.

Kevin Garnett at the 1998 All-Star Game.

Kevin's a big star among Timberwolves fans and he's becoming a national one as well. He has a national advertising campaign for Nike where he is the chief of the "Fun Police."

Kevin's favorite place to be, however, is on the basketball court. He led the Timberwolves to their most wins in team history with 45 in 1997-98.

Behind Kevin's season average of 18.5 points, 9.6 rebounds, 4.2 assists, 1.83 blocks, and 1.7 steals the Timberwolves were in the playoffs for the second year in a row.

Kevin and the Timberwolves met the heavily favored Seattle SuperSonics in the first round. The Sonics came out and destroyed the Timberwolves by 25 points. Most people thought the Timberwolves would be swept out of the playoffs in three lopsided games. Kevin and his team, however, had other ideas. The Timberwolves shocked the Sonics by beating them in Game 2—in Seattle!

The series moved to Minnesota where Kevin rocked the Target Center with thunderous dunks, blocked shots, and clutch baskets. The Timberwolves grabbed another win, 98-90.

The veteran SuperSonics bounced back and won Game 4 and Game 5 in hard-fought, close games to take the series. The exhausted, injured, and young Timberwolves played their hearts out with only seven players available for action.

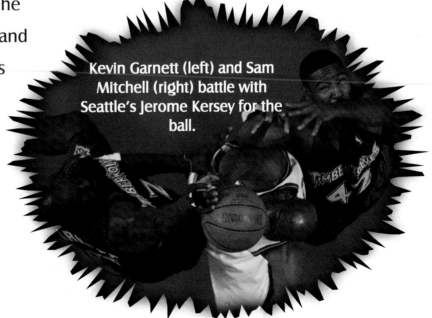

Kevin Garnett (left) and Sam Mitchell (right) battle with Seattle's Jerome Kersey for the ball.

The Sky's the Limit

After the hard-fought playoff series, Sonics superstar Gary Payton said, "The Timberwolves are going to be unbelievable. With Garnett, Marbury, and that energy, the sky's the limit."

Even though Garnett was exhausted after the Game 5 loss he wanted to get right back on the court. "I can't wait to start practicing," he said. "This just pumped me up. I'm ready for next year already."

While Kevin is a grown-up on the basketball court, at home he's still a kid. He likes to play video games, listen to music, and watch

'Da Kid' is 'Da Man' to Minnesota Timberwolves fans.

basketball. In the off-season he still visits his hometown of Mauldin. His hometown is proud of him. His high school jersey number, 21, was retired in 1996.

He also gives back to his hometown. He helped get the basketball court resurfaced at Springfield Park, where he had spent so many hours playing basketball.

When he's in Mauldin, he plays basketball with his friends and with kids from the high school. After the games they might get something to eat, and Kevin tells them about life in the NBA.

"It's not that easy. I know that now," he said. "It's not just accepting the money, the chance to play in the pros. It's accepting the responsibility of playing in a man's league."

The Sonics' Detlef Schrempf watches as Garnett towers above him with a jump shot during the 1998 playoffs.

Kevin's Stats

Profile

Born: May 19, 1976, in South Carolina

High School: Farragut Academy (Chicago, Il)

Drafted: NBA, 1995, first round (fifth overall), by Minnesota Timberwolves

Height: 6-feet, 11-inches

Weight: 220 pounds

Garnett grabs
a rebound.

**Garnett goes for
the big slam.**

Honors

1995-96

Named to the NBA All-Rookie Second
Team

Broke club record for blocked shots in a
season, with 131

1996-97

Appears in NBA All-Star Game

Broke team single-season record for
blocked shots with 163.

Finished first among forwards in the NBA
with 2.12 blocks per game.

1997-98

Starter in NBA All-Star Game

Leads the Timberwolves to their best
season ever and their first playoff win.

Chronology

May 19, 1976 - Born in South Carolina.

1993 - Began to attract attention from college coaches during his junior year at Mauldin High School.

1994 - Led Mauldin Mavericks to upper-state championship game in March.
- Amateur Athletic Union team won Kentucky Hoopfest summer tournament.
- Family moved to Chicago in September. Kevin attended Farragut Academy for his senior year in high school.

1995 - Helped Farragut win 28 of its first 29 games. The team won the Chicago Public League tournament and reached the Final 8 of the Class AA state tournament.
- Named to the all-tournament team.
- Selected as Illinois' "Mr. Basketball."
- MVP of the McDonald's High School All-American Game.
- Selected by the Minnesota Timberwolves in the NBA draft.

1996 - Named to the NBA's All-Rookie Second Team.

1997 - Appeared in the NBA All-Star Game.
- Averaged 17.3 points a game in his first playoff series appearance.
- Signed a six-year contract extension for $125 million—the highest contract in sports history.

1998 - Started in the NBA All-Star Game.

Glossary

ASSIST - A pass to a teammate who makes a basket.

DUNK - To slam a ball through the basket.

JUMP SHOT (jumper) - Shooting the ball while jumping into the air.

LAYUP - A shot released near the basket, usually while moving toward the basket.

NATIONAL BASKETBALL ASSOCIATION (NBA) - A group of teams competing at the highest level of professional basketball.

OVERTIME - An extra period played if the score is tied at the end of regulation time.

PLAYOFFS - Games played after the regular season to determine the champion.

REBOUND - To grab the ball after a missed shot.

SCREEN - To stand in the way of an opponent, blocking his progress so a teammate can get open.

STATE TOURNAMENT - A series of games after the regular season to determine the state champion.

Index